BEHAVIORAL INTERVIEW QUESTIONS AND ANSWERS

CHETAN SINGH

Made with ♥ on the Notion Press Platform
www.notionpress.com

Contents

Acknowledgements

I would like to take a moment to express my deepest gratitude to everyone who has supported me in writing this book, "Behavioral Interview Questions and Answers."

First and foremost, I would like to thank my family and friends for their unwavering love and encouragement throughout the writing process. Their support has been a constant source of inspiration and motivation.

I also extend my heartfelt appreciation to the team at the publishing house for their guidance and expertise in bringing this book to life. Their editorial input and attention to detail have been invaluable.

I would like to acknowledge the numerous professionals in the field of human resources and recruitment who have generously shared their insights and expertise with me. Your contributions have helped to make this book a comprehensive guide to behavioral interview questions and answers.

Finally, I want to express my gratitude to the readers of this book. It is my sincere hope that the information presented here will be helpful to you in your job search and career development. Your feedback and support are greatly appreciated.

CHAPTER ONE

I. Introduction

Behavioral interview questions have become a popular method for assessing job candidates during the hiring process. Unlike traditional interview questions that focus on skills and experience, behavioral questions are designed to uncover a candidate's past behavior in specific situations. The belief is that past behavior is a good predictor of future behavior. Behavioral interview questions are often open-ended and require a candidate to provide a detailed response that includes specific examples of their behavior in a given situation.

The purpose of this book is to provide a comprehensive guide to behavioral interview questions and answers. In this book, you will learn what behavioral interview questions are, why they are important, and how to prepare for them. You will also find a list of key behavioral interview questions and sample answers to help you prepare for your next interview.

Whether you are a recent college graduate, an experienced professional looking for a new job, or someone who is returning to the workforce after a break, this book will help you navigate the behavioral interview process with confidence. By the end of this book, you will have a solid understanding of how to answer behavioral interview questions and increase your chances of landing the job of your dreams.

A. Purpose of the book

The purpose of this book is to provide a comprehensive guide to behavioral interview questions and answers. The book is designed to help job seekers understand what behavioral interview questions are, why they are important, and how to prepare for them. The book will also provide a list of key behavioral interview questions and sample answers to help job seekers prepare for their next interview.

The book is intended for anyone who is preparing for a job interview, whether they are a recent college graduate, an experienced professional looking for a new job, or someone who is returning to the workforce after a break. The book will help job seekers navigate the behavioral interview process with confidence and increase their chances of landing the job of their dreams.

In short, the purpose of this book is to help job seekers prepare for behavioral interview questions, understand what employers are looking for in candidates, and ultimately, get hired for their desired position.

B. Importance of Behavioral Interview Questions

Behavioral interview questions are important because they provide employers with insights into a candidate's past behavior and decision-making skills. Traditional interview questions that focus on skills and experience can only tell an employer so much about a candidate. By contrast, behavioral interview questions can help employers understand how a candidate has acted in specific situations and how they are likely to behave in the future.

Behavioral interview questions are also valuable because they can help employers assess a candidate's soft skills. Soft skills, such as communication, problem-solving, and teamwork, are often critical to success in many jobs, but they can be difficult to assess through traditional interview questions or a candidate's resume. Behavioral interview questions can help employers evaluate a candidate's soft skills by asking them to provide examples of how they have used those skills in the past.

In addition, behavioral interview questions can help employers identify red flags in a candidate's behavior or decision-making. For example, if a candidate struggles to provide examples of how they have handled difficult situations or has a history of poor communication with coworkers, those could be warning signs to an employer.

Overall, the importance of behavioral interview questions lies in their ability to provide employers with more comprehensive and accurate information about a candidate's past behavior, soft skills, and decision-making abilities. This information can help employers make more informed hiring decisions and ultimately, lead to better job matches and increased job satisfaction for both the employer and the employee.

C. What to expect in the book

In this book, you can expect to find a comprehensive guide to behavioral interview questions and answers.

First, you will learn what behavioral interview questions are and why they are important. You will understand the different types of behavioral interview questions and how to prepare for them.

Next, you will find a list of key behavioral interview questions that are commonly asked during job interviews. For each question, you will see examples of what the interviewer is looking for and how to structure your response using the STAR method (Situation, Task, Action, Result).

The book will also provide tips and best practices for answering behavioral interview questions, including how to be specific and detailed in your answers, using positive language, and focusing on the outcome.

To further help you prepare, the book will provide sample answers to each of the key behavioral interview questions. These sample answers will demonstrate how to apply the STAR method and provide a framework for structuring your own responses.

Finally, the book will conclude with a summary of the key points and a final advice section for job seekers. Additionally, the book will provide additional resources for those looking to further their understanding of behavioral interview questions and continue to develop their interview skills.

Overall, this book will provide a comprehensive and practical guide for anyone preparing for a job interview that involves behavioral interview questions.

CHAPTER TWO

II. Understanding Behavioral Interview Questions

Behavioral interview questions are a type of interview question that focuses on a candidate's past behavior in specific situations. The purpose of these questions is to understand how a candidate has behaved in the past, which can give an indication of how they might behave in the future.

Behavioral interview questions are designed to be open-ended and often begin with phrases such as "Tell me about a time when..." or "Describe a situation where..." The questions are intended to elicit a detailed response from the candidate, which should include specific examples of their behavior in the given situation.

One key feature of behavioral interview questions is that they often require a candidate to use the STAR method to structure their response. The STAR method stands for Situation, Task, Action, and Result. In response to a behavioral interview question, a candidate should describe the situation or task they faced, explain the actions they took to address the situation, and then describe the result of their actions.

Employers use behavioral interview questions to assess a candidate's soft skills, such as communication, problem-solving, teamwork, and decision-making. Behavioral interview questions are considered more reliable than traditional interview questions because they provide concrete examples of a candidate's behavior rather than relying on hypothetical situations or generalizations.

Overall, understanding behavioral interview questions is essential for anyone preparing for a job interview, as these questions are commonly asked during the interview process and can have a significant impact on the hiring decision. By understanding what behavioral interview questions are and how to prepare for them, candidates can increase their chances of success in the job interview process.

A. Definition of Behavioral Interview Questions

Behavioral interview questions are a type of interview question that focuses on a candidate's past behavior in specific situations. These questions are designed to assess a candidate's soft skills, such as communication, problem-solving, teamwork, and decision-making, by asking them to provide specific examples of how they have used these skills in the past.

Behavioral interview questions are open-ended and typically begin with phrases such as "Tell me about a time when..." or "Describe a situation where..." The questions are intended to elicit a detailed response from the candidate, which should include specific examples of their behavior in the given situation.

The STAR method is often used to structure a candidate's response to a behavioral interview question. The STAR method stands for Situation, Task, Action, and Result. In response to a behavioral interview question, a candidate should describe the situation or task they faced, explain the actions they took to address the situation, and then describe the result of their actions.

Employers use behavioral interview questions to gain insights into a candidate's past behavior and decision-making skills, which can help them assess a candidate's fit for the job and the company culture. Behavioral interview questions are considered more reliable than traditional interview questions because they provide concrete examples of a candidate's behavior rather than relying on hypothetical situations or generalizations.

Overall, behavioral interview questions are an important part of the job interview process, and understanding how to prepare for and answer these questions can increase a candidate's chances of success in landing their desired job.

A. Types of Behavioral Interview Questions

There are several types of behavioral interview questions that an employer may ask during a job interview. These questions are designed to assess a candidate's soft skills and past behavior in specific situations.

Problem-solving questions: These questions are designed to assess a candidate's ability to identify and solve problems. Examples of problem-solving questions include "Tell me about a time when you had to solve a complex problem at work" or "Describe a situation where you had to make a tough decision."

Teamwork questions: These questions are designed to assess a candidate's ability to work collaboratively with others. Examples of teamwork questions include "Tell me about a time when you had to work with a difficult team member" or "Describe a situation where you had to resolve a conflict with a co-worker."

Leadership questions: These questions are designed to assess a candidate's ability to lead and manage others. Examples of leadership questions include "Tell me about a time when you had to lead a team to accomplish a difficult task" or "Describe a situation where you had to provide feedback to a team member."

Communication questions: These questions are designed to assess a candidate's ability to communicate effectively with others. Examples of communication questions include "Tell me about a time when you had to communicate a complex idea to a non-technical audience" or "Describe a situation where you had to deal with a difficult customer."

Adaptability questions: These questions are designed to assess a candidate's ability to adapt to change and new situations. Examples of adaptability questions include "Tell me about a time when you had to adapt to a new work environment" or "Describe a situation where you had to change your approach to a project due to unexpected circumstances."

Overall, understanding the different types of behavioral interview questions can help candidates prepare for their job interview and provide specific examples that demonstrate their skills and experience.

C. How to prepare for Behavioral Interview Questions

Preparing for behavioral interview questions involves several steps that can help candidates demonstrate their skills and experience effectively. Here are some tips for preparing for behavioral interview questions:

- Research the company: Understanding the company culture and values can help candidates anticipate the types of behavioral interview questions that may be asked. Candidates can research the company's website, social media pages, and news articles to gain insights into the company's mission and vision.

- Review the job description: Carefully reviewing the job description can help candidates identify the specific soft skills and qualifications that are required for the job. Candidates can use this information to prepare specific examples that demonstrate their relevant experience and skills.
- Practice using the STAR method: The STAR method is a useful framework for answering behavioral interview questions. Candidates can practice using this method to structure their responses and provide specific examples of their past behavior.
- Prepare a list of examples: Candidates can prepare a list of examples that demonstrate their relevant skills and experience. These examples should be specific and detailed and should highlight the candidate's actions and results.
- Anticipate common questions: Candidates can anticipate common behavioral interview questions and prepare responses in advance. Some common questions include "Tell me about a time when you had to deal with a difficult customer" or "Describe a situation where you had to work with a difficult team member."
- Practice with a friend or mentor: Practicing with a friend or mentor can help candidates feel more confident and comfortable answering behavioral interview questions. Candidates can also receive feedback on their responses and identify areas where they may need to improve.

Overall, preparing for behavioral interview questions involves researching the company, reviewing the job description, practicing using the STAR method, preparing examples, anticipating common questions, and practicing with a friend or mentor. By following these steps, candidates can increase their chances of success in the job interview process.

CHAPTER THREE

III. Key Behavioral Interview Questions

While there is no definitive list of behavioral interview questions that employers may ask, there are some common questions that candidates can prepare for. Here are some key behavioral interview questions that candidates may encounter:

- Tell me about a time when you had to solve a problem: This question is designed to assess a candidate's problem-solving skills and ability to think critically. Candidates should provide specific examples of a problem they faced, their thought process in addressing the problem, and the outcome of their actions.
- Describe a situation where you had to work with a difficult team member: This question is designed to assess a candidate's ability to work collaboratively with others. Candidates should provide specific examples of a difficult team member they had to work with, the steps they took to address the situation and the outcome of their actions.
- Tell me about a time when you had to deal with a difficult customer: This question is designed to assess a candidate's customer service skills and ability to handle challenging situations. Candidates should provide specific examples of a difficult customer they had to deal with, how they addressed the customer's concerns, and the outcome of their actions.
- Describe a situation where you had to adapt to a new work environment: This question is designed to assess a candidate's adaptability and ability to handle change. Candidates should provide specific examples of a new work environment they had to adapt to, how they adapted to the new environment and the outcome of their actions.

- Tell me about a time when you had to provide feedback to a team member: This question is designed to assess a candidate's leadership and communication skills. Candidates should provide specific examples of a team member they had to provide feedback to, how they approached the situation, and the outcome of their actions.
- Describe a situation where you had to meet a tight deadline: This question is designed to assess a candidate's time management and organizational skills. Candidates should provide specific examples of a tight deadline they had to meet, how they managed their time, and the outcome of their actions.

Overall, understanding these key behavioral interview questions and preparing specific examples to demonstrate relevant skills and experience can help candidates succeed in the job interview process.

A. Communication Skills

Communication skills are an essential aspect of many jobs, and employers often ask behavioral interview questions to assess a candidate's communication skills. Here are some key behavioral interview questions related to communication skills:

- Tell me about a time when you had to communicate effectively with a team: This question is designed to assess a candidate's ability to work collaboratively and communicate effectively with others. Candidates should provide specific examples of a project or task they worked on with a team, how they communicated with team members and the outcome of their actions.
- Describe a situation where you had to present information to a group: This question is designed to assess a candidate's public speaking and presentation skills. Candidates should provide specific examples of a presentation they gave, how they prepared for the presentation and the outcome of their actions.
- Tell me about a time when you had to explain a complex concept to someone: This question is designed to assess a candidate's ability to communicate complex ideas clearly and concisely. Candidates should provide specific examples of a complex concept they had to explain, how they approached the situation, and the outcome of their actions.

- Describe a situation where you had to communicate bad news to a coworker or client: This question is designed to assess a candidate's ability to handle difficult situations and communicate sensitive information effectively. Candidates should provide specific examples of a situation where they had to deliver bad news, how they approached the situation, and the outcome of their actions.
- Tell me about a time when you had to resolve a conflict through communication: This question is designed to assess a candidate's conflict resolution skills and ability to communicate effectively in challenging situations. Candidates should provide specific examples of a conflict they resolved through communication, how they approached the situation and the outcome of their actions.

Overall, by preparing specific examples that demonstrate their communication skills, candidates can increase their chances of success in the job interview process.

1. **Examples Based Question and Answer**

Question: Give an example of a time when you had to communicate difficult information to a team member or customer

Answer: here's an example of a time when I had to communicate difficult information to a team member:

- In my previous job, I was working on a project with a colleague, and we had a tight deadline to meet. However, my colleague had been struggling to keep up with the workload and was falling behind on their tasks. I knew that we wouldn't be able to meet the deadline if we didn't address the issue, so I decided to have a conversation with my colleague.
- I scheduled a meeting with my colleague to discuss the project's progress and expressed my concerns about the deadline. I asked my colleague if they needed any additional support or resources to complete their tasks. My colleague initially denied needing any help, but as we continued to talk, they opened up about feeling overwhelmed and stressed.
- I listened actively to my colleague's concerns and suggested some strategies to help them manage their workload better. We also agreed to adjust the project timeline to give my colleague more time to complete their tasks.

Although the conversation was difficult, it was essential to address the issue and find a solution to ensure the project's success. By communicating openly and honestly with my colleague, we were able to work together to overcome the challenges and complete the project successfully.

Question: Describe a situation where you had to persuade someone to see things your way

Answer: here's an example of a situation where I had to persuade someone to see things my way:

- In my previous job, I was working as a marketing manager for a consumer products company, and we were launching a new product. As part of the launch plan, I proposed a marketing campaign that I believed would be effective in reaching our target audience and generating sales. However, one of my colleagues, who was a senior executive, disagreed with my approach and had a different idea.
- To persuade my colleague to see things my way, I decided to present a detailed analysis of the market research data, which supported my proposed campaign. I prepared a presentation that showcased the target audience's demographics, psychographics, and behavior, and demonstrated how my campaign would align with their preferences and needs. I also included examples of similar successful campaigns from other companies in our industry.
- During the presentation, I used persuasive language and emphasized the benefits of my approach, such as increased revenue and brand awareness. I also addressed any potential concerns or objections that my colleague might have had and provided solutions to mitigate them.
- After the presentation, my colleague was convinced that my proposed campaign was the better approach, and we moved forward with it. The campaign was a success and achieved the desired results.
- In this situation, I used persuasive communication and evidence-based arguments to persuade my colleague to see things my way. By presenting a logical and compelling case, I was able to gain their buy-in and achieve a successful outcome.

B. Teamwork

Teamwork is a critical aspect of many jobs, and employers often ask behavioral interview questions to assess a candidate's ability to work collaboratively with others. Here are some key behavioral interview questions related to teamwork:

- Describe a time when you had to work with a difficult team member: This question is designed to assess a candidate's ability to work effectively with others, even in challenging situations. Candidates should provide specific examples of a difficult team member they worked with, how they approached the situation, and the outcome of their actions.
- Tell me about a time when you had to collaborate with a diverse group of people: This question is designed to assess a candidate's ability to work well with people from diverse backgrounds and perspectives. Candidates should provide specific examples of a situation where they worked with people from different cultures, ethnicities, or work styles, how they approached the situation and the outcome of their actions.
- Describe a situation where you had to lead a team: This question is designed to assess a candidate's leadership skills and ability to guide and motivate a team. Candidates should provide specific examples of a situation where they led a team, how they approached the situation, and the outcome of their actions.
- Tell me about a time when you had to take on extra responsibilities to help a team member: This question is designed to assess a candidate's willingness to help others and their commitment to teamwork. Candidates should provide specific examples of a situation where they took on extra responsibilities to support a team member, how they approached the situation, and the outcome of their actions.
- Describe a situation where you had to resolve a conflict within a team: This question is designed to assess a candidate's conflict resolution skills and ability to work through challenging situations within a team. Candidates should provide specific examples of a conflict within a team they resolved, how they approached the situation and the outcome of their actions.

Overall, by preparing specific examples that demonstrate their ability to work collaboratively with others, candidates can increase their chances of success in the job interview process.

1. Tell me about a time when you had to resolve a conflict with a team member

Sure, I can provide an example of a time when I had to resolve a conflict with a team member:

- In my previous job, I worked on a project with a team of three other colleagues. One of my team members, let's call him John, had a different work style than the rest of us. He preferred to work independently and often missed deadlines, causing delays in the project timeline. This caused frustration and tension within the team.
- To resolve the conflict with John, I decided to approach him in a calm and professional manner. I scheduled a one-on-one meeting with him to discuss the issue and understand his perspective. During the meeting, I listened actively to his concerns and suggested potential solutions, such as setting clear expectations and deadlines and providing more support and resources.
- After the meeting, I followed up with an email outlining our discussion and the action items we agreed on. I also made a point to check in with John regularly to provide feedback and ensure that he was on track.
- As a result of our conversation and the action items we put in place, John became more communicative and responsive, and we were able to complete the project on time. The conflict was resolved, and the team was able to work more effectively together.

In this situation, I used active listening, problem-solving, and communication skills to resolve the conflict with John. By approaching the situation in a professional and collaborative manner, I was able to find a solution that benefited the entire team.

1. Describe an instance where you had to collaborate with someone from a different department or team

Sure, I can provide an example of a time when I had to collaborate with someone from a different department or team:

- In my previous job, I worked as a software engineer in the development team. We were tasked with developing a new feature for our company's e-commerce platform that required integrating with the payment processing system, which was maintained by the finance team.

- To collaborate with the finance team, I scheduled a meeting with the project manager and the lead developer from the finance team. During the meeting, we discussed the project requirements, the technical specifications, and the timeline for delivery. We also identified potential risks and issues and discussed how to address them.
- To ensure effective collaboration and communication, we established a regular meeting cadence and created a shared project plan with clear milestones and deadlines. We also set up a Slack channel to facilitate real-time communication and provide updates on the project's progress.
- Throughout the project, we worked closely together, with regular check-ins and updates. We also made sure to celebrate our successes and address any challenges as they arose.
- As a result of our collaboration, we were able to deliver the new feature on time and within budget. The feature was well-received by customers and generated significant revenue for the company.

In this situation, I used communication, collaboration, and problem-solving skills to work effectively with a team from a different department. By establishing clear lines of communication and setting expectations upfront, we were able to work together seamlessly and achieve our goals.

C. Problem-Solving and Decision-Making

Sure, I can provide an example of a time when I had to use problem-solving and decision-making skills:

- In my previous job as a product manager, we received customer feedback that our product's user interface was confusing and difficult to navigate. After conducting user research and analyzing the data, we identified several areas where we could improve the user experience.
- To address this problem, I formed a cross-functional team consisting of designers, engineers, and user researchers. We brainstormed potential solutions and evaluated them based on their feasibility, impact, and resource requirements.
- After several rounds of ideation and prototyping, we narrowed down the options to two possible solutions. To make a final decision, we conducted

a usability test with a sample of our target audience and analyzed the results.

- Based on the test results and feedback from the team, we decided to implement a new navigation structure that was more intuitive and user-friendly. We created a project plan with clear milestones and deadlines and assigned tasks to each team member.
- Throughout the implementation process, we conducted regular testing and made adjustments based on user feedback. We also communicated updates and progress to stakeholders and received their feedback and support.
- As a result of our problem-solving and decision-making efforts, we were able to improve the user experience and received positive feedback from customers. The product's usability score increased, and we saw a significant increase in user engagement and retention.

In this situation, I used problem-solving and decision-making skills to address customer feedback and improve the product's user experience. By collaborating with a cross-functional team and using data-driven insights, we were able to identify and implement a successful solution.

1. Give an example of a time when you had to make a decision with limited information

Sure, here's an example of a time when I had to make a decision with limited information:

- In my previous job as a project manager, we were tasked with developing a new product feature for our company's e-commerce platform. We had a tight deadline, and the feature required significant technical expertise, which was outside my area of expertise.
- To address this challenge, I met with the development team and the stakeholders to understand the project requirements and the technical specifications. However, I realized that I had limited knowledge of the technical details required to make a decision.
- To overcome this, I identified a subject matter expert within the company who had experience with the technology required for the project. I set up a meeting with the expert, explained the project requirements, and asked for advice on how to proceed.

- Based on the expert's advice, I made a decision to proceed with a specific approach for the project. I communicated the decision to the development team and stakeholders, and we began working on the project.
- As the project progressed, we encountered some unexpected technical challenges that required us to modify our approach. However, by using an agile development process, we were able to adapt to the changes and complete the project on time.

In this situation, I had to make a decision with limited technical knowledge by seeking advice from a subject matter expert. By leveraging the expert's knowledge and experience, I was able to make an informed decision and successfully complete the project.

2. Tell me about a time when you had to solve a complex problem

Sure, here's an example of a time when I had to solve a complex problem:

- In my previous job as a data analyst, we received a request from a client to analyze a large data set and identify patterns and trends that could help improve their business performance. The data set was large and unstructured, and it required significant data cleaning and transformation before we could analyze it.
- To address this challenge, I collaborated with a team of data scientists and software engineers to develop a data processing pipeline that could clean and transform the data automatically. We used a combination of Python scripts and data analysis tools to automate the process and ensure that the data was clean and ready for analysis.
- After cleaning and transforming the data, we used various statistical techniques and machine learning algorithms to identify patterns and trends in the data. We also visualized the data using interactive dashboards and reports to help the client understand the insights.
- As we analyzed the data, we discovered several complex relationships and correlations that required additional analysis and validation. We conducted additional tests and sensitivity analyses to ensure that our insights were accurate and actionable.
- After several weeks of analysis and collaboration, we were able to identify several key insights that helped the client improve their

business performance. Our recommendations led to a significant increase in their sales and revenue, and the client was highly satisfied with our work.

In this situation, I had to solve a complex problem by collaborating with a team of experts and using advanced data analysis techniques. By developing a data processing pipeline and using statistical and machine learning algorithms, we were able to uncover insights that helped the client improve their business performance.

D. Leadership

Sure, here's an example of a time when I demonstrated leadership:

- In my previous job as a team leader, we were tasked with developing a new software product for a client. The project was complex and required a high level of technical expertise and collaboration between different teams.
- As the team leads, I realized that one of the critical challenges we faced was ensuring that everyone understood their roles and responsibilities and had the necessary resources to complete their tasks.
- To address this challenge, I scheduled a series of meetings with each team member to discuss their role in the project and identify any areas where they needed additional support or resources. I also set up a project management system that allowed us to track progress and identify any issues in real time.
- As the project progressed, we encountered several unexpected challenges that required us to adapt our approach. I encouraged the team to brainstorm solutions and come up with creative ideas to overcome the challenges.
- I also made sure to communicate regularly with the client to keep them informed of our progress and address any concerns they had.
- By leveraging my leadership skills, we were able to successfully complete the project on time and within budget. The client was highly satisfied with our work and praised our team's collaborative approach and attention to detail.

In this situation, I demonstrated leadership by ensuring that everyone understood their roles and responsibilities and had the necessary support and resources to complete their tasks. I also encouraged collaboration and creativity to overcome unexpected challenges and communicated regularly with the client to ensure their satisfaction.

1. Describe a situation where you had to lead a team through a difficult project

Certainly, here's an example of a situation where I had to lead a team through a difficult project:

- In my previous job as a project manager, we were tasked with developing a new software product for a client within a tight deadline. The project involved several teams, including software development, quality assurance, and project management.
- As the project manager, I realized that the key to success was effective communication, collaboration, and coordination between the different teams. I organized regular meetings to update the team on the project's progress, discuss any issues, and identify any areas where we needed additional resources or support.
- As we progressed through the project, we encountered several challenges that required us to adapt our approach. One significant challenge was when one of our team members had to leave the project unexpectedly due to personal reasons. This left us with a significant skills gap that threatened to delay the project.
- To address this challenge, I worked with the team to identify alternative resources and found a consultant who could fill the skills gap. I also reorganized the project timeline and tasks to accommodate the consultant's availability and ensure that we could deliver the project on time.
- Throughout the project, I made sure to stay in close communication with the client, providing regular updates and addressing any concerns they had promptly. I also encouraged the team to collaborate and share ideas to overcome challenges and find innovative solutions.
- By leveraging my leadership skills, we were able to complete the project within the deadline and to the client's satisfaction. The team felt motivated and engaged throughout the project, and we were able to build

strong relationships and teamwork.

In this situation, I had to lead a team through a difficult project by emphasizing effective communication, collaboration, and coordination between different teams. I also adapted the project timeline and tasks to accommodate unexpected challenges and identified alternative resources when necessary. By staying in close communication with the client and encouraging teamwork, we were able to complete the project successfully.

2. Tell me about a time when you had to make a tough decision as a leader

Sure, here's an example of a time when I had to make a tough decision as a leader:

- In my previous job as a department head, we were faced with a challenging situation when one of our team members was repeatedly absent from work without a valid reason. The team member's absence was starting to affect the team's productivity and morale.
- As the department head, I had to make a tough decision on how to handle the situation. I scheduled a meeting with the team member to discuss their absences and to understand their reasons for being absent from work.
- During the meeting, the team member revealed that they were dealing with personal issues that had impacted their mental health and ability to come to work. While I was sympathetic to their situation, I knew that I had to consider the impact of their absences on the team and the organization as a whole.
- After considering all the factors, I decided that the best course of action was to offer the team member a temporary leave of absence to focus on their mental health and well-being. I also arranged for the team member to receive support and counseling during their absence.
- While it was a tough decision to make, I knew that it was the right thing to do for both the team member and the organization. The team member was grateful for the support and understanding, and their return to work was a positive one for the team's productivity and morale.

In this situation, I had to make a tough decision as a leader by balancing the team member's personal situation with the impact of their absence on the team and the organization. By offering a temporary leave of absence and arranging for support and counseling, I was able to support the team member while maintaining the team's productivity and morale.

CHAPTER FOUR

IV. How to Answer Behavioral Interview Questions

Here are some tips on how to answer behavioral interview questions:

- Use the STAR method: When answering behavioral interview questions, use the STAR (Situation, Task, Action, Result) method. Start by describing the situation, task, or challenge you faced, explain the actions you took, and end with the result or outcome of your actions.
- Be specific: Provide specific details about the situation or project you are describing. Use numbers, facts, and figures to make your answers more impactful.
- Focus on your role: Make sure your answers focus on your specific role in the situation. Describe the actions you took and how they contributed to the outcome.
- Highlight your skills: Use your answers to highlight the skills and qualities that make you a strong candidate for the position.
- Be honest: Be honest in your answers, even if the situation or outcome was not ideal. Employers want to see how you handle challenges and learn from mistakes.
- Practice: Practice answering behavioral interview questions ahead of time. This can help you feel more confident and prepared during the actual interview.
- Listen carefully: Listen carefully to the interviewer's questions and make sure you understand what they are asking. If you're unsure, ask for clarification before answering.

Overall, the key to answering behavioral interview questions is to provide specific, honest, and relevant examples that demonstrate your skills and abilities. By using the STAR method and focusing on your role in each situation, you can provide strong, impactful answers that showcase your strengths as a candidate.

A. STAR Method

1. What is the STAR Method?

The STAR method is a structured approach for answering behavioral interview questions. It stands for Situation, Task, Action, and Result. Here's how to use the STAR method:

- Situation: Describe the situation or challenge you faced. This sets the context for your answer and helps the interviewer understand the scenario.
- Task: Explain the task or goal you were trying to accomplish. This should be specific and measurable, so the interviewer can understand the objective of the situation.
- Action: Describe the actions you took to address the situation or accomplish the task. This is the most important part of your answer because it demonstrates your skills and abilities.
- Result: Share the outcome of your actions. Be specific and use metrics if possible to show the impact of your actions.

2. How to use the STAR Method

Here's an example of how to use the STAR method to answer a behavioral interview question:

- Question: "Tell me about a time when you had to solve a complex problem."
- Answer using the STAR method:
- Situation: In my previous role, we had a production line shut down due to a malfunctioning machine.
- Task: My task was to identify the cause of the malfunction and get the line back up and running as quickly as possible.
- Action: I started by reviewing the machine's manual and consulting with our maintenance team. After determining that the issue was with a faulty sensor, I worked with our procurement team to quickly order a replacement part. While we waited for the part to arrive, I organized a

team to work on other parts of the production line that were not affected by the malfunction.

- Result: With my team's efforts, we were able to quickly replace the faulty sensor and get the production line back up and running within 24 hours. By keeping the line operational during this downtime, we minimized the impact on our production schedule and prevented any major delays in delivering our products to customers.

Using the STAR method can help you structure your answers in a way that is clear and concise. It also helps you provide specific examples that demonstrate your skills and abilities, which can be very effective in showcasing your suitability for the job.

B. Tips for Answering Behavioral Interview Questions

Here are some tips for answering behavioral interview questions:

- Be specific: When answering behavioral interview questions, use specific examples to illustrate your skills and experiences. Avoid giving general or hypothetical answers.
- Use the STAR method: As mentioned earlier, the STAR method is a useful way to structure your answers to behavioral interview questions. By following this method, you can provide a clear and concise answer that highlights your skills and experiences.
- Show your thought process: In addition to describing what you did, explain why you did it. This shows that you can think critically and make informed decisions.
- Emphasize your role: When describing a situation, make sure to highlight your specific role and responsibilities. This helps the interviewer understand your level of involvement and contribution.
- Use positive language: Use positive language to describe your experiences, actions, and results. Avoid negative language or blaming others for problems.
- Practice beforehand: To prepare for a behavioral interview, think of specific examples from your work experience that demonstrate your skills and abilities. Practice telling these stories using the STAR method.

- Be honest: Be truthful in your answers and don't exaggerate your experiences or skills. It's better, to be honest about your limitations and show a willingness to learn and improve.
- Listen carefully: Listen carefully to the interviewer's questions and make sure you understand what they are asking. If you're not sure, ask for clarification.
- Stay focused: Stay focused on the question being asked and avoid going off on tangents. Keep your answers concise and to the point.

By following these tips, you can provide strong, specific, and effective answers to behavioral interview questions. This can help you stand out to the interviewer and increase your chances of getting the job.

Here are some more tips for answering behavioral interview questions:

1. Be specific and detailed

here are some more specific and detailed tips for answering behavioral interview questions:

- Use numbers and metrics: Whenever possible, use numbers and metrics to quantify your achievements and accomplishments. For example, instead of saying "I improved sales," say "I increased sales by 25% over a six-month period."
- Focus on the positive: When describing difficult situations, focus on how you overcame challenges and achieved a positive outcome. Instead of dwelling on the negative aspects of the situation, emphasize the steps you took to resolve the issue.
- Use action verbs: When describing your actions and accomplishments, use strong action verbs to make your story more compelling. For example, instead of saying "I worked on a team project," say "I collaborated with a team of six to develop a new marketing strategy."
- Provide context: When describing a situation, provide enough context so that the interviewer understands the background and context of the situation. This helps them understand the scope and complexity of the problem you were facing.
- Be concise: While it's important to be specific and detailed, it's also important to be concise. Avoid rambling or going off on tangents. Stick to the main point and focus on answering the question being asked.

- Use examples from different contexts: Try to provide examples from different contexts and situations. This demonstrates that you have a range of skills and experiences and can adapt to different situations.
- Show growth and development: If you encountered a difficult situation in the past and made a mistake, use it as an opportunity to demonstrate growth and development. Talk about what you learned from the experience and how you've applied that knowledge to future situations.

By following these specific and detailed tips, you can provide strong, compelling, and effective answers to behavioral interview questions.

2. Use positive language

Yes, using positive language is an important aspect of answering behavioral interview questions effectively. Here are some tips for using positive language in your answers:

- Emphasize your strengths: Instead of focusing on your weaknesses or limitations, focus on your strengths and what you bring to the table. Use positive language to describe your skills, experience, and accomplishments.
- Avoid negative language: Avoid using negative language such as "I can't" or "I didn't" and instead use positive language such as "I can" or "I have." This helps to create a positive impression and demonstrates a can-do attitude.
- Be enthusiastic: Show enthusiasm and passion for the work you do and the experiences you've had. This helps to create a positive and engaging conversation with the interviewer.
- Highlight your achievements: Use positive language to describe your achievements and accomplishments. Focus on the positive outcomes and impact you've had in previous roles.
- Express a positive attitude: Show a positive attitude and approach to work. Use language that conveys a can-do attitude and a willingness to learn and grow.

By using positive language, you can create a positive and engaging conversation with the interviewer and demonstrate your strengths and positive qualities. This can help to make a strong and positive impression during the interview.

3. Focus on the outcome

Yes, focusing on the outcome is an important aspect of answering behavioral interview questions effectively. Here are some tips for focusing on the outcome in your answers:

- Emphasize the results: When describing a situation, focus on the results and outcomes you achieved. Use language that highlights the positive impact you had in previous roles.
- Quantify your achievements: Use numbers and metrics to quantify your achievements and accomplishments. For example, if you increased sales, mention the percentage increase and the timeframe.
- Show the impact: Emphasize the impact you had on the team or organization. Demonstrate how your actions and decisions made a positive impact on the project or team's overall success.
- Use positive language: Use positive language to describe the outcome and results you achieved. This helps to create a positive impression and demonstrates your ability to achieve positive outcomes.
- Tie the outcome to the question: Make sure that the outcome you describe is directly tied to the question being asked. This helps to demonstrate that you are actively listening and addressing the interviewer's concerns.

By focusing on the outcome in your answers, you can demonstrate your ability to achieve positive results and make a positive impact in your previous roles. This can help to create a strong and positive impression during the interview.

CHAPTER FIVE

V. Sample Answers to Behavioral Interview Questions

Question: Tell me about a time when you had to handle a difficult situation with a customer

Answer: In my previous role as a customer service representative, I had a customer who was very upset about a billing issue. I listened to their concerns and tried to understand their perspective. I apologized for the inconvenience and explained the steps we would take to resolve the issue. I kept the customer informed throughout the process and followed up to ensure they were satisfied with the resolution. As a result, the customer was happy with the outcome and continued to do business with us.

Question: Describe a situation where you had to work with a difficult team member

Answer: In a previous project, I had a team member who was very resistant to change and had a negative attitude. I tried to understand their concerns and addressed their questions and doubts. I also ensured that I communicated clearly and openly with them to avoid any misunderstandings. Additionally, I tried to recognize their contributions to the project and provided positive feedback when they performed well. By doing this, I was able to build a positive relationship with the team member and we were able to work collaboratively towards the project's goals.

Question: Give an example of a time when you had to make a tough decision

Answer: In a previous role, I had to make a tough decision about a vendor that we had been working with for several years. The vendor's quality had been declining, and they were not meeting our expectations. After careful consideration, I recommended that we terminate our relationship with the vendor and find a new supplier. This was a tough decision because we had a long-standing relationship with the vendor, but it was necessary to ensure that we met our quality standards and maintained our customer satisfaction. In the end, the decision was the right one and our customers were happy with the improved quality of our products.

Question: Tell me about a time when you had to lead a team through a difficult project.

Answer: In my previous role as a project manager, I had a team working on a project that had a very tight deadline and complex requirements. I made sure that everyone was clear on the goals and expectations, and provided the team with the resources and support they needed to succeed. I also monitored progress closely and identified any roadblocks early on. I encouraged collaboration and open communication, and worked with the team to find creative solutions to challenges. Through effective leadership and teamwork, we were able to complete the project on time and deliver high-quality results.

These sample answers demonstrate the STAR method of answering behavioral interview questions and highlight specific examples of situations and outcomes. Remember to be specific and detailed, use positive language, and focus on the outcome to create strong and effective answers.

CHAPTER SIX

VI. Interview Based Behavioral Interview Questions and Answers

Behavioral interview questions are commonly used by hiring managers to assess a candidate's past behavior in certain situations, which can be an indicator of how they might behave in future situations. Here are some common behavioral interview questions and examples of answers:

Tell me about a time when you had to handle a difficult situation with a co-worker.

Example answer: "In my previous job, I had a co-worker who was consistently negative and difficult to work with. Rather than letting the situation escalate, I approached the co-worker and asked if we could have a private conversation to discuss our working relationship. During the conversation, I listened to their concerns and provided feedback on how we could work better together. By the end of the conversation, we were able to come to an understanding and work more effectively as a team."

Can you tell me about a time when you had to adapt to a new situation?

Example answer: "In my previous job, we were implementing a new software system which required a significant change in our workflows. I knew it would take some time for everyone to adjust, so I took the initiative to provide training and support to my colleagues to help them navigate the new system. By doing so, we were able to minimize the impact on our productivity and ensure a smooth transition."

Tell me about a time when you had to solve a complex problem.

Example answer: "In my previous role, we had a customer who had a complex issue that required a solution involving multiple teams. I took the lead in coordinating with each team and ensured that we were all aligned in our approach. Through collaboration and effective communication, we were able to solve the problem and deliver a solution to the customer that exceeded their expectations."

Can you tell me about a time when you had to work under pressure to meet a deadline?

Example answer: "In my previous job, we had a project with a tight deadline and a lot of competing priorities. To ensure that we met the deadline, I worked with my team to prioritize tasks and set clear expectations for each team member. I also communicated with stakeholders to ensure that everyone was aware of the progress we were making. By working collaboratively and staying focused, we were able to complete the project on time and deliver high-quality results."

Tell me about a time when you had to handle a dissatisfied customer.

Example answer: "In my previous role, we had a customer who was dissatisfied with our product. I listened to their concerns and apologized for the inconvenience. I then worked with my team to identify the root cause of the issue and came up with a solution that would address the customer's concerns. Through open communication and a willingness to go above and beyond, we were able to turn the dissatisfied customer into a loyal one."

Can you tell me about a time when you had to make a difficult decision?

Example answer: "In my previous job, we had to decide whether to invest in a new product line. After conducting thorough research and analyzing the data, I presented my findings to the team and made a recommendation to move forward with the investment. Although it was a difficult decision, it ultimately led to increased revenue and growth for the company."

Tell me about a time when you had to work with a team to accomplish a goal.

Example answer: "In my previous role, we had a project that required input from multiple departments. I took the lead in coordinating with each team and delegating tasks to ensure that everyone was working towards the same goal. By leveraging everyone's strengths and working collaboratively, we were able to complete the project on time and exceed our objectives."

Can you tell me about a time when you had to provide constructive feedback to a colleague?

Example answer: "In my previous job, I noticed that a colleague was consistently arriving late to meetings and missing deadlines. I approached the colleague and provided feedback on how their behavior was impacting the team and the company. I also offered suggestions on how they could improve their time management skills and stay on top of their responsibilities. By providing constructive feedback, we were able to improve the colleague's performance and strengthen our team dynamic."

Tell me about a time when you had to handle a crisis situation.

Example answer: "In my previous role, we had a major system outage that impacted our customers. I took the lead in communicating with the affected customers and provided regular updates on our progress in resolving the issue. I also worked with our technical team to quickly diagnose and fix the problem. By staying calm under pressure and taking swift action, we were able to restore service and minimize the impact on our customers."

Can you tell me about a time when you had to take initiative to solve a problem?

Example answer: "In my previous job, we had a process that was causing inefficiencies and delays. I took the initiative to identify the root cause of the problem and proposed a solution to my supervisor. After getting buy-in, I worked with my team to implement the new process, which resulted in a significant increase in productivity and cost savings for the company."

Remember, when answering behavioral interview questions, it's important to provide specific examples and demonstrate how your actions led to positive outcomes. Use the STAR method to structure your answers (Situation, Task, Action, Result) and be prepared to provide additional details if the interviewer asks for clarification.

Tell me about a time when you had to prioritize competing tasks.

Example answer: "In my previous job, I was responsible for managing multiple projects simultaneously. To prioritize competing tasks, I created a detailed project plan and broke down each task into smaller, manageable steps. I then assigned each task a priority level and focused on completing the most urgent tasks first. By staying organized and managing my time effectively, I was able to complete all of the projects on time and exceed our goals."

Can you tell me about a time when you had to persuade someone to change their opinion?

Example answer: "In my previous role, we had a disagreement with a client over a project proposal. I took the initiative to listen to the client's concerns and present alternative solutions that addressed their needs. Through effective communication and a willingness to understand the client's perspective, we were able to come to an agreement that satisfied both parties and resulted in a successful project outcome."

Tell me about a time when you had to demonstrate leadership skills.

Example answer: "In my previous job, I was tasked with leading a team of colleagues on a complex project. To demonstrate my leadership skills, I set clear goals and expectations, provided regular feedback and support, and recognized the team's accomplishments. By providing direction and support, I was able to inspire and motivate the team to achieve our objectives and deliver high-quality results."

Can you tell me about a time when you had to overcome a setback or failure?

Example answer: "In my previous role, I made a mistake on a project that led to delays and cost overruns. I took responsibility for the mistake and worked with my team to come up with a plan to address the issue. Through effective communication and a commitment to fixing the problem, we were able to recover from the setback and deliver the project on time and within budget."

Tell me about a time when you had to manage a difficult customer.

Example answer: "In my previous job, I had a customer who was dissatisfied with our product and was becoming increasingly difficult to work with. I took the initiative to listen to their concerns, empathize with their situation, and provide solutions to address their needs. By demonstrating a commitment to customer service and going above and beyond, we were able to turn the situation around and retain the customer's business."

Can you tell me about a time when you had to work with a difficult colleague?

Example answer: "In my previous job, I had a colleague who was frequently unresponsive to emails and missed deadlines. I took the initiative to schedule a meeting with the colleague to discuss our concerns and find a solution. By approaching the situation with empathy and a willingness to collaborate, we were able to identify the root cause of the colleague's behaviour and come up with a plan to improve communication and meet our shared goals."

Tell me about a time when you had to adapt to a new situation or environment.

Example answer: "In my previous role, I was assigned to a new project that required me to work with a team of colleagues from different departments. To adapt to the new situation, I took the initiative to learn more about each colleague's strengths and weaknesses and find ways to leverage their skills to achieve our goals. By adapting to the new environment and being open to new ideas and perspectives, we were able to successfully complete the project and deliver high-quality results."

Can you tell me about a time when you had to learn a new skill or technology quickly?

Example answer: "In my previous job, I was assigned to a project that required me to learn a new programming language within a short timeframe. To quickly learn the new skill, I took advantage of online resources and tutorials, and practiced coding on my own time. By being proactive and diligent in my learning, I was able to successfully complete the project and deliver high-quality results."

Tell me about a time when you had to work under pressure or tight deadlines.

Example answer: "In my previous role, we had a project that required us to complete a large amount of work within a tight deadline. To handle the pressure, I created a detailed project plan and broke down each task into smaller, manageable steps. I also communicated regularly with my team to ensure that everyone was on track and meeting their deadlines. By staying organized and focused, we were able to successfully complete the project on time and exceed our goals."

Can you tell me about a time when you had to resolve a conflict with a colleague or customer?

Example answer: "In my previous job, I had a customer who was dissatisfied with the service they received and demanded a refund. I took the initiative to listen to their concerns and address their needs. By demonstrating empathy and a commitment to customer service, we were able to resolve the conflict and retain the customer's business. I also worked with my team to identify areas for improvement and make changes to prevent similar conflicts from arising in the future."

Can you tell me about a time when you had to work with a team to achieve a goal?

Example answer: "In my previous role, we were tasked with developing a new product for a client within a tight timeframe. I worked with a team of colleagues from different departments to develop a project plan, allocate tasks, and establish regular communication channels. By working collaboratively and leveraging each team member's strengths, we were able to successfully deliver the product on time and within budget."

Tell me about a time when you had to take a calculated risk.

Example answer: "In my previous job, we had a new client who wanted to try a new marketing strategy that was untested in our industry. I took the initiative to research the strategy, identify potential challenges, and develop a plan to mitigate the risks. By taking a calculated risk and being proactive in my approach, we were able to successfully implement the new strategy and achieve significant results."

Can you tell me about a time when you had to deliver difficult feedback to a colleague or subordinate?

Example answer: "In my previous role, I had a team member who was consistently underperforming. I took the initiative to schedule a meeting with the team member to discuss their performance and provide feedback on areas for improvement. By being direct, empathetic, and providing actionable solutions, we were able to turn the situation around and improve the team member's performance."

Tell me about a time when you had to navigate a complex or ambiguous situation.

Example answer: "In my previous job, we had a project that had many unknown variables and required frequent adjustments to the plan. To navigate the complex situation, I established clear communication channels with my team and stakeholders, researched and evaluated different options, and developed a contingency plan in case of unexpected challenges. By being proactive and adaptable, we were able to successfully complete the project and exceed our goals."

Can you tell me about a time when you had to mentor or train a colleague or subordinate?

Example answer: "In my previous role, I was tasked with training a new team member on our company's software system. To ensure their success, I developed a comprehensive training plan, provided ongoing support and feedback, and encouraged open communication. By investing time and energy in their development, I was able to help the team member become proficient in the software system and contribute to the team's success."

Tell me about a time when you had to manage a difficult project.

Example answer: "In my previous role, we were tasked with implementing a new software system for a client with a tight deadline. The project was complex, and we faced several challenges, including issues with the software and delays in receiving client feedback. To manage the difficult project, I established clear communication channels with my team and the client, developed a contingency plan, and worked diligently to identify and address potential roadblocks. By being proactive and adaptable, we were able to complete the project on time and within budget."

Can you tell me about a time when you had to handle a difficult customer or stakeholder?

Example answer: "In my previous role, we had a customer who was unhappy with our service and threatened to take their business elsewhere. I took the initiative to listen to the customer's concerns, address their needs, and develop a plan to improve their experience. By demonstrating empathy and a commitment to customer service, we were able to retain the customer's business and earn their trust."

Tell me about a time when you had to make a difficult decision.

Example answer: "In my previous job, we were faced with a difficult decision regarding whether to pursue a new project that had a high level of risk but also a significant potential reward. After conducting extensive research and analysis, I presented my findings to the team and recommended that we move forward with the project. By making a well-informed decision and considering all factors, we were able to successfully complete the project and achieve our goals."

Can you tell me about a time when you had to work with limited resources?

Example answer: "In my previous role, we had a project that required us to work with limited resources, including a small budget and a limited number of team members. To maximize our resources, I developed a detailed project plan, leveraged technology, and automation to streamline tasks, and worked closely with my team to ensure that everyone was contributing effectively. By being creative and resourceful, we were able to successfully complete the project and exceed our goals."

Tell me about a time when you had to implement a change in a process or procedure.

Example answer: "In my previous job, we identified an issue with our customer onboarding process that was causing delays and negatively impacting our customers' experience. I took the initiative to research the issue, identify potential solutions, and work with my team to implement a new onboarding process. By being proactive and open to change, we were able to improve the process and create a better experience for our customers."

Can you tell me about a time when you had to collaborate with a colleague or team member who had a different working style than yours?

Example answer: "In my previous job, I had to work with a colleague who had a different working style than mine. While I preferred to take a more structured approach, my colleague was more spontaneous and preferred to work on tasks as they came up. To collaborate effectively, we established clear communication channels, identified each other's strengths and weaknesses, and divided tasks based on our respective preferences. By being flexible and adapting to each other's working styles, we were able to successfully complete the project and achieve our goals."

Tell me about a time when you had to resolve a conflict with a coworker.

Example answer: "In my previous job, I had a conflict with a coworker regarding a project we were working on. To resolve the conflict, I scheduled a meeting with my coworker to discuss our perspectives and identify the root of the issue. We actively listened to each other's concerns, developed a plan to address the issue, and established clear expectations for future communication. By working collaboratively and finding common ground, we were able to resolve the conflict and work effectively together."

Can you tell me about a time when you had to deal with a difficult or unexpected change in your work environment?

Example answer: "In my previous role, we had a sudden change in leadership that resulted in a significant shift in our team's priorities and responsibilities. To adapt to the change, I took the initiative to research and understand the new leadership's vision, communicate with my team to clarify expectations, and identify potential challenges and opportunities. By being proactive and adaptable, we were able to successfully navigate the change and achieve our goals."

Tell me about a time when you had to prioritize multiple tasks or projects with competing deadlines.

Example answer: "In my previous job, I had multiple tasks and projects with competing deadlines that required me to prioritize effectively. To manage the workload, I developed a system to prioritize tasks based on their importance and urgency, established clear communication channels with my team and stakeholders, and delegated tasks when appropriate. By being organized and proactive, I was able to successfully manage multiple projects and meet all deadlines."

Can you tell me about a time when you had to learn a new skill or technology quickly?

Example answer: "In my previous role, we had to quickly learn and implement a new software system to support our business operations. To learn the new technology quickly, I leveraged online resources and tutorials, attended training sessions, and worked with my team to identify best practices and challenges. By being proactive and collaborative, we were able to learn the new technology quickly and effectively integrate it into our workflow."

Can you tell me about a time when you had to make a difficult decision with limited information?

Example answer: "In my previous job, I had to make a difficult decision regarding a project with limited information available. To approach the situation, I gathered as much information as possible from various sources, consulted with my team and stakeholders, and analyzed the potential risks and benefits of each decision. I also identified potential scenarios and developed contingency plans in case the decision did not yield the desired results. By being thorough and proactive, I was able to make an informed decision and mitigate potential risks."

Tell me about a time when you had to work under pressure to meet a tight deadline.

Example answer: "In my previous role, we had a project with a tight deadline that required me to work under pressure. To meet the deadline, I created a detailed timeline and schedule, prioritized tasks based on importance and urgency, and communicated frequently with my team and stakeholders to ensure everyone was on the same page. I also made sure to take breaks and practice stress-management techniques to avoid burnout. By being organized and focused, I was able to complete the project on time and deliver high-quality results."

Can you tell me about a time when you had to overcome a significant challenge or obstacle?

Example answer: "In my previous job, we faced a significant challenge when a key team member left unexpectedly in the middle of a critical project. To overcome the obstacle, I stepped up and took on additional responsibilities, worked with my team to redistribute tasks and priorities, and communicated frequently with stakeholders to keep them updated on our progress. I also identified opportunities to streamline processes and improve communication to prevent similar challenges in the future. By being adaptable and collaborative, we were able to successfully complete the project and achieve our goals."

Tell me about a time when you had to provide constructive feedback to a coworker or team member.

Example answer: "In my previous job, I had to provide constructive feedback to a team member regarding their performance on a project. To approach the situation, I scheduled a one-on-one meeting with the team member to discuss specific areas of improvement and identified ways to support their growth and development. I also made sure to provide positive feedback and acknowledge their strengths to balance the feedback. By being empathetic and focused on growth, I was able to provide constructive feedback that helped the team member improve and succeed."

Can you tell me about a time when you had to take initiative and go above and beyond your job duties to achieve a goal?

Example answer: "In my previous role, we had a project with a tight deadline that required additional resources to complete. To take initiative and go above and beyond my job duties, I identified areas where I could contribute beyond my current responsibilities, communicated with my team and stakeholders to offer my assistance, and worked longer hours and weekends to complete the project on time. By being proactive and committed to the team's success, we were able to achieve our goals and deliver high-quality results."

Can you tell me about a time when you had to resolve a conflict with a coworker or team member?

Example answer: "In my previous job, I had a conflict with a coworker regarding a project's approach. To resolve the conflict, I scheduled a one-on-one meeting with the coworker to listen to their concerns, shared my perspective and identified common ground, and worked collaboratively to find a solution that incorporated both our ideas. We also established clear communication and expectations moving forward to prevent similar conflicts in the future. By being respectful and focused on finding a mutually beneficial solution, we were able to resolve the conflict and maintain a positive working relationship."

Tell me about a time when you had to adapt to a new situation or change.

Example answer: "In my previous role, we had a change in leadership that resulted in a shift in priorities and processes. To adapt to the new situation, I stayed open-minded, asked questions to clarify expectations and objectives, and worked collaboratively with my team and stakeholders to identify opportunities and challenges. I also took advantage of training and development opportunities to improve my skills and knowledge in areas that were relevant to the new direction. By being adaptable and proactive, I was able to successfully transition to the new situation and achieve our goals."

Can you tell me about a time when you had to persuade someone to see things your way?

Example answer: "In my previous job, I had to persuade a stakeholder to adopt a new approach to a project. To persuade them, I conducted research and provided data to support my argument, listened to their concerns and addressed them directly, and presented a clear and compelling case for why the new approach would be beneficial. I also followed up with the stakeholder to address any additional questions or concerns they had. By being prepared and persuasive, I was able to successfully convince the stakeholder to adopt the new approach and achieve our goals."

Tell me about a time when you had to delegate tasks to others effectively.

Example answer: "In my previous job, we had a project with multiple tasks that required delegation. To delegate tasks effectively, I identified team members' strengths and weaknesses, communicated clearly and concisely what was expected of each team member, set clear deadlines and provided support and feedback throughout the process. I also established open communication channels to address any challenges or issues that arose. By being organized and supportive, I was able to delegate tasks effectively and achieve our goals."

Can you tell me about a time when you had to think creatively to solve a problem?

Example answer: "In my previous role, we faced a problem where we needed to reduce costs without sacrificing quality. To think creatively, I worked collaboratively with my team to identify areas where we could streamline processes, reduce waste, and optimize resources. We also researched new technologies and tools that could help us achieve our goals. By being innovative and collaborative, we were able to develop a new approach that reduced costs while maintaining high-quality standards."

Tell me about a time when you had to take initiative to solve a problem without being asked.

Example answer: "In my previous job, we had a project deadline that was rapidly approaching, and it became clear that we were going to miss it. I took the initiative to investigate the cause of the delay, identified bottlenecks in the process, and proposed a new plan that would help us meet the deadline. I also communicated my plan to my team and got their feedback, adjusted it accordingly, and presented it to our supervisor. By taking the initiative, we were able to complete the project on time and avoid any negative consequences."

Can you tell me about a time when you had to deal with a difficult customer or client?

Example answer: "In my previous role as a customer service representative, I had a customer who was frustrated with our company's service. To deal with the difficult customer, I listened actively to their concerns, apologized for any inconvenience they experienced, and asked questions to better understand the situation. I then worked collaboratively with my team and the customer to find a solution that would meet their needs. By being empathetic and proactive, I was able to turn the situation around and leave the customer satisfied."

Tell me about a time when you had to handle a high-pressure situation.

Example answer: "In my previous job, we had a client presentation that was crucial to the success of our project. During the presentation, our equipment malfunctioned, and we had to improvise to complete the presentation. To handle the high-pressure situation, I kept my composure, assessed the situation, and identified alternative solutions quickly. I also communicated with my team to ensure that everyone was on the same page and worked collaboratively to make the presentation a success. By remaining calm and focused, we were able to impress the client and achieve our goals."

Can you tell me about a time when you had to give constructive feedback to a colleague?

Example answer: "In my previous job, I had to give constructive feedback to a colleague who was consistently arriving late for meetings. To give the feedback effectively, I scheduled a private meeting with my colleague and used specific examples to illustrate the issue. I also offered suggestions and resources to help my colleague improve their punctuality, and we agreed on a plan to monitor progress moving forward. By being clear and supportive, I was able to give the feedback effectively, and my colleague was able to improve their behavior."

Tell me about a time when you had to admit to making a mistake and how you handled it.

Example answer: "In my previous job, I made a mistake that impacted the project timeline. To handle the mistake, I took responsibility for it, acknowledged the impact it had on the team, and communicated with my supervisor and team members to develop a plan to address the issue. I also learned from the mistake by identifying what led to it and taking steps to prevent it from happening again in the future. By taking responsibility and being proactive, I was able to turn the mistake into a learning opportunity and regain the trust of my team."

Can you tell me about a time when you had to work with a difficult coworker or teammate?

Example answer: "In my previous job, I had a coworker who was very negative and resistant to change. To work effectively with this coworker, I first tried to understand their perspective and their reasons for being negative. I then worked to build a positive relationship with them by finding common ground and highlighting areas of agreement. I also communicated effectively by actively listening, being respectful, and using positive language. By taking the time to understand and work with this difficult coworker, I was able to build a positive working relationship and achieve our team's goals."

Tell me about a time when you had to adapt to a new situation or environment.

Example answer: "In my previous job, I was part of a team that was transitioning to a new software system. To adapt to the new situation, I took the initiative to learn the new system by attending training sessions, reviewing online resources, and seeking out advice from colleagues who had experience with the system. I also communicated with my team to ensure that we were all on the same page and worked collaboratively to troubleshoot any issues that arose. By being proactive and adaptable, I was able to help my team transition smoothly to the new software system."

Can you tell me about a time when you had to persuade someone to see your point of view?

Example answer: "In my previous job, I had to persuade a team member to adopt a new strategy for our project. To persuade them, I first listened actively to their concerns and objections and acknowledged their perspective. I then presented my point of view and provided evidence and data to support my argument. I also communicated the benefits of the new strategy and showed how it aligned with our team's goals. By being clear, convincing, and respectful, I was able to persuade my team member to adopt the new strategy and achieve our project goals."

Tell me about a time when you had to take on a new responsibility or task outside of your job description.

Example answer: "In my previous job, I took on a new responsibility when our team leader went on extended leave. To take on the new responsibility, I first identified the gaps in our team's workflow and prioritized the tasks that needed attention. I then communicated with my team to ensure that everyone was on the same page and worked collaboratively to fill the gaps in the workflow. I also reached out to other departments for support and resources and kept our team leader informed of our progress. By taking on the new responsibility and working collaboratively, our team was able to maintain our workflow and meet our goals."

Can you tell me about a time when you had to resolve a conflict with a coworker or teammate?

Example answer: "In my previous job, I had a conflict with a coworker over a project deadline. To resolve the conflict, I first listened actively to my coworker's concerns and acknowledged their perspective. I then presented my perspective and provided evidence to support my argument. We also worked collaboratively to find a solution that would meet both of our needs and the project deadline. By being open to feedback, finding common ground, and being proactive in finding a solution, we were able to resolve the conflict and complete the project successfully."

Tell me about a time when you had to deal with a difficult customer or client.

Example answer: "In my previous job, I had to deal with a difficult customer who was unhappy with a product they received. To deal with the situation, I first listened actively to their concerns and empathized with their frustration. I then worked to find a solution that would meet their needs and the company's policies. I communicated effectively by being clear, respectful, and responsive to their questions and concerns. By being proactive and focused on finding a solution, I was able to turn the situation around and earn the customer's satisfaction."

Can you tell me about a time when you had to prioritize multiple tasks or projects with competing deadlines?

Example answer: "In my previous job, I had to prioritize multiple tasks with competing deadlines when our team was short-staffed. To prioritize the tasks, I first assessed the urgency and importance of each task and identified any dependencies or constraints. I then communicated with my team and stakeholders to ensure that we were all aligned on the priorities and timelines. I also took the initiative to delegate tasks and seek out resources to support the workload. By being proactive and strategic in my approach, I was able to prioritize the tasks effectively and meet the deadlines."

Tell me about a time when you had to work under pressure to meet a tight deadline.

Example answer: "In my previous job, I had to work under pressure to meet a tight deadline for a project. To meet the deadline, I first assessed the scope and requirements of the project and identified any risks or challenges. I then developed a detailed project plan with specific timelines and milestones and communicated it to my team and stakeholders. I also worked collaboratively with my team to ensure that we were all aligned on the project goals and progress. By being organized, focused, and communicative, we were able to meet the tight deadline and deliver the project successfully."

Can you tell me about a time when you had to think creatively to solve a problem?

Example answer: "In my previous job, we had a problem with our customer satisfaction scores declining. To solve the problem, I first assessed the root causes and identified the areas where we could improve. I then brainstormed creative solutions with my team, such as implementing a customer feedback program and developing a training program for our customer service team. I also communicated with our stakeholders to ensure that they were supportive of our initiatives. By thinking creatively and collaboratively, we were able to improve our customer satisfaction scores and maintain a positive reputation."

Tell me about a time when you had to make a difficult decision.

Example answer: "In my previous job, I had to make a difficult decision when we had to lay off a team member due to budget cuts. To make the decision, I first assessed the impact on our team and the company and gathered input from our stakeholders. I then weighed the options and considered the long-term implications of each decision. I also communicated with our team member in a respectful and empathetic manner and provided support and resources to help them transition. By being thoughtful, decisive, and empathetic, I was able to make the difficult decision in the best interest of our team and company."

Can you tell me about a time when you had to adapt to a new situation or change?

Example answer: "In my previous job, I had to adapt to a new situation when our team was assigned a new project with a different scope and timeline. To adapt to the situation, I first assessed the project requirements and identified any gaps in our team's skills or resources. I then communicated with my team and stakeholders to ensure that we were all aligned on the project goals and timeline. I also took the initiative to learn new skills and techniques that would help us to be more efficient and effective in our work. By being adaptable and proactive, we were able to successfully complete the project on time and within budget."

Tell me about a time when you had to handle a difficult colleague or team member.

Example answer: "In my previous job, I had to handle a difficult colleague who was not meeting their performance expectations. To handle the situation, I first gathered data and feedback from their team members and stakeholders to better understand the root causes of the problem. I then had a candid conversation with the colleague, providing specific examples of where they were falling short and outlining the expectations for improvement. I also provided support and resources to help them address their performance issues, such as additional training or coaching. By being direct and supportive, we were able to turn around their performance and improve team morale."

Can you tell me about a time when you had to collaborate with a diverse group of people?

Example answer: "In my previous job, I had to collaborate with a diverse group of people on a cross-functional project. To collaborate effectively, I first recognized the unique strengths and perspectives of each team member and worked to leverage them for the project's success. I also established clear communication channels and processes to ensure that everyone was informed and aligned on the project's goals and progress. I also took the initiative to address any conflicts or challenges that arose and worked collaboratively with my team to find solutions. By being inclusive and collaborative, we were able to successfully complete the project and build strong relationships across our organization."

Tell me about a time when you had to take ownership of a project or initiative.

Example answer: "In my previous job, I had to take ownership of a project to streamline our customer onboarding process. To take ownership, I first assessed the current process and identified the areas where we could improve. I then developed a detailed project plan with specific timelines and milestones and communicated it to my team and stakeholders. I also took the initiative to collaborate with our cross-functional teams, such as marketing and customer service, to ensure that we were aligned on the project goals and approach. By taking ownership and being proactive, we were able to successfully streamline the onboarding process and improve customer satisfaction."

Can you tell me about a time when you had to learn a new skill or technology?

Example answer: "In my previous job, I had to learn a new technology when our company switched to a new customer relationship management (CRM) system. To learn the technology, I first assessed my current skills and identified any gaps in my knowledge. I then took advantage of the resources provided by our company, such as online training and user guides, to learn the new technology. I also collaborated with my team members who had more experience with the technology to gain additional insights and best practices. By being proactive and committed to learning, I was able to successfully adapt to the new technology and contribute to our team's success."

Tell me about a time when you had to manage a difficult customer or client.

Example answer: "In my previous job, I had to manage a difficult client who was unhappy with our services. To manage the situation, I first listened to the client's concerns and empathized with their frustration. I then provided them with a clear and actionable plan to address their issues and ensured that they had a dedicated point of contact for ongoing support. I also followed up regularly with the client to check in on their progress and address any additional concerns that arose. By being proactive and communicative, I was able to successfully resolve the client's issues and improve their satisfaction with our services."

Can you tell me about a time when you had to make a difficult decision with limited information?

Example answer: "In my previous job, I had to make a difficult decision with limited information when our company was considering a major investment in a new technology platform. To make the decision, I first gathered as much information as possible from industry research, competitor analysis, and internal data. I then worked collaboratively with our cross-functional teams, such as finance and operations, to identify the potential risks and benefits of the investment. Despite the limited information, I made a decision based on the available data and my judgment, weighing the potential risks and benefits. By being analytical and decisive, we were able to make a successful investment in the new technology platform."

Tell me about a time when you had to delegate tasks to others.

Example answer: "In my previous job, I had to delegate tasks to others when our team was working on a complex project with multiple deadlines. To delegate tasks effectively, I first assessed the skills and strengths of each team member and assigned tasks that aligned with their strengths. I also provided clear instructions and expectations for each task and ensured that each team member had the necessary resources and support to complete their tasks effectively. I also followed up regularly with each team member to check on their progress and address any issues that arose. By delegating tasks effectively, we were able to complete the project on time and within budget."

Can you tell me about a time when you had to work under pressure to meet a deadline?

Example answer: "In my previous job, I had to work under pressure to meet a deadline when our team was assigned a high-priority project with a tight deadline. To work effectively under pressure, I first established clear priorities and timelines for each task and communicated them to my team members. I also identified any potential risks or obstacles that could impact our ability to meet the deadline and worked proactively to mitigate them. I also maintained a positive and focused attitude, keeping my team motivated and focused on the project goals. By working effectively under pressure, we were able to successfully complete the project on time and meet our client's expectations."

Tell me about a time when you had to resolve a conflict with a colleague or team member.

Example answer: "In my previous job, I had to resolve a conflict with a team member who had a different approach to a project than I did. To resolve the conflict, I first listened to their perspective and tried to understand their reasoning. I then shared my own perspective and explained why I believed my approach would be more effective. We then worked collaboratively to find a compromise that incorporated the strengths of both approaches. By being open-minded and collaborative, we were able to resolve the conflict and complete the project successfully."

Can you tell me about a time when you had to learn a new skill quickly?

Example answer: "In my previous job, I had to learn a new software program quickly in order to complete a project for a client. To learn the new skill, I first identified the resources available to me, such as online tutorials and training materials. I also asked colleagues who were proficient in the software for tips and advice. I then practiced using the software regularly and sought feedback from colleagues and supervisors to ensure I was on the right track. By being proactive and committed to learning, I was able to quickly become proficient in the software and complete the project successfully."

Tell me about a time when you had to take initiative to solve a problem.

Example answer: "In my previous job, I noticed that our team was experiencing communication breakdowns that were impacting our productivity. To solve the problem, I took the initiative to organize a team meeting to discuss the issue openly and identify potential solutions. During the meeting, I facilitated a constructive discussion and helped identify strategies for improving communication, such as using clear and concise messaging and setting regular check-ins. By taking the initiative to address the problem, we were able to improve our communication and productivity as a team."

Can you tell me about a time when you had to adapt to a new work environment?

Example answer: "In my previous job, I had to adapt to a new work environment when our team moved to a new office location. To adapt to the new environment, I first familiarized myself with the new office layout and resources, such as the location of supplies and equipment. I also made an effort to get to know my new colleagues and build relationships with them. I asked for feedback on my work and actively sought out opportunities to collaborate with others. By being proactive and open-minded, I was able to quickly adapt to the new work environment and become an integral part of the team."

Tell me about a time when you had to collaborate with colleagues from different departments.

Example answer: "In my previous job, I had to collaborate with colleagues from different departments to complete a project for a client. To collaborate effectively, I first established clear lines of communication and established a shared understanding of the project goals and timelines. I also identified the strengths and expertise of each team member and assigned tasks accordingly. I facilitated regular check-ins and worked proactively to address any issues or roadblocks that arose during the project. By collaborating effectively with colleagues from different departments, we were able to complete the project successfully and meet the client's expectations."

Can you tell me about a time when you had to admit a mistake and take responsibility for it?

Example answer: "In my previous job, I made a mistake in a report that I submitted to my supervisor. I realized my mistake after the report had already been distributed to several stakeholders. To take responsibility for my mistake, I immediately alerted my supervisor to the error and offered to help correct it. I also contacted the stakeholders who had received the report to apologize for the mistake and provide them with the corrected information. By taking responsibility for my mistake and proactively addressing it, I was able to maintain the trust and respect of my supervisor and colleagues."

Tell me about a time when you had to persuade someone to see your point of view.

Example answer: "In my previous job, I had to persuade a colleague to adopt a new approach to a project we were working on. Initially, my colleague was resistant to the idea, but I understood that the new approach would ultimately benefit the project and our team's goals. To persuade my colleague, I first listened to their concerns and objections to the new approach. I then presented the benefits of the new approach, including its potential to save time and resources and improve the project's outcome. I also shared examples of how the new approach had been successful in similar projects. By being patient and empathetic, while also presenting a compelling argument, I was able to persuade my colleague to adopt the new approach."

Can you tell me about a time when you had to work under pressure to meet a deadline?

Example answer: "In my previous job, I had to work under pressure to meet a tight deadline for a client project. To manage the pressure, I first broke down the project into smaller tasks and established clear timelines for each task. I also communicated regularly with my colleagues and supervisor to ensure everyone was aware of the project's progress and any issues or challenges that arose. I worked extra hours and weekends to ensure the project was completed on time, but I also made sure to take breaks and practice self-care to manage the stress. By being organized, communicative, and diligent, I was able to meet the deadline successfully."

Tell me about a time when you had to work with someone you didn't get along with.

Example answer: "In my previous job, I had to work with a colleague who had a different working style than my own, and we didn't always see eye-to-eye on certain issues. To manage the situation, I first made an effort to understand my colleague's perspective and priorities. I also communicated clearly and respectfully with them, even when we disagreed. I tried to find common ground and identify areas where we could work together effectively. By being respectful, communicative, and collaborative, I was able to build a productive working relationship with my colleague, even though we didn't always agree."

Can you tell me about a time when you had to manage a conflict with a colleague?

Example answer: "In my previous job, I had to manage a conflict with a colleague who disagreed with my approach to a project. To manage the conflict, I first listened to my colleague's concerns and tried to understand their perspective. I then communicated my own perspective and explained my reasoning for my approach. I tried to find common ground and identify areas where we could compromise. We also involved our supervisor to provide a neutral perspective and help us find a solution that worked for both of us. By being patient, respectful, and collaborative, we were able to manage the conflict effectively and complete the project successfully."

Tell me about a time when you had to make a difficult decision with incomplete information.

Example answer: "In my previous job, I had to make a difficult decision about whether to proceed with a project based on incomplete information about the client's budget and timeline. To make the decision, I first consulted with my supervisor and colleagues to get their input and perspectives. I also did additional research to try to fill in the gaps in my knowledge. Ultimately, I made the decision to proceed with the project based on the available information, but I also set up regular check-ins and contingency plans to ensure we could adjust if new information emerged. By being proactive, consultative, and flexible, I was able to make a difficult decision with incomplete information."

Tell me about a time when you had to adapt to a new situation or environment.

Example answer: "In my previous job, I was transferred to a new department that had a completely different work culture and team dynamic than I was used to. To adapt to the new situation, I first observed and listened to my new colleagues to understand their expectations and work styles. I also asked questions and sought feedback to ensure I was meeting the team's needs. I made an effort to be flexible and adaptable, taking on new tasks and responsibilities as needed. By being open-minded and willing to learn, I was able to adapt to the new situation and build strong relationships with my new colleagues."

Can you tell me about a time when you had to provide constructive feedback to a colleague or team member?

Example answer: "In my previous job, I had to provide constructive feedback to a team member who was consistently falling behind on their tasks and missing deadlines. To provide the feedback, I first approached the conversation from a place of empathy and understanding, acknowledging that the team member may be facing challenges or obstacles that I wasn't aware of. I then provided specific examples of the team member's behavior and the impact it was having on the team and project. I also worked with the team member to develop an action plan to improve their performance and provided ongoing support and encouragement. By being compassionate and solution-focused, I was able to provide constructive feedback that helped the team member improve their performance."

Tell me about a time when you had to work with a difficult client or customer.

Example answer: "In my previous job, I had to work with a difficult client who was dissatisfied with the work we had done for them. To manage the situation, I first listened to the client's concerns and tried to understand their perspective. I then communicated our own perspective and explained the work we had done and why we believed it met their needs. I also worked with the client to identify areas where we could make improvements or adjustments to better meet their needs. By being patient, communicative, and proactive, I was able to turn the situation around and build a stronger working relationship with the client."

Can you tell me about a time when you had to innovate or come up with a creative solution to a problem?

Example answer: "In my previous job, we were faced with a challenge where a client needed a product delivered much sooner than our typical turnaround time. To meet the client's needs, I proposed a new workflow that involved utilizing a new software tool and streamlining our production process. I also worked with my colleagues to ensure everyone was trained and comfortable with the new workflow. By being innovative and proactive, we were able to deliver the product to the client ahead of schedule and exceed their expectations."

Tell me about a time when you had to learn a new skill or technology quickly.

Example answer: "In my previous job, we implemented a new software tool that was critical to our workflow. Although I had some experience with similar tools, I still had to learn the new software quickly to ensure we could use it effectively. To learn the new software, I first watched tutorials and read documentation to gain a basic understanding of its functionality. I also set up practice scenarios and tested the software in a safe environment to get comfortable with its features. I asked questions and sought feedback from my colleagues to ensure I was using the software correctly. By being proactive and diligent, I was able to learn the new skill quickly and help my team use the software effectively."

Can you tell me about a time when you had to work collaboratively with a team to achieve a goal?

Example answer: "In my previous job, we had a project where we had to work collaboratively with multiple departments to achieve our goal. To ensure effective collaboration, I first established clear communication channels and defined each department's roles and responsibilities. I also organized regular meetings to review progress and discuss any challenges or obstacles. By being proactive and collaborative, we were able to identify and resolve any issues quickly, work seamlessly across departments, and deliver a successful project."

Tell me about a time when you had to prioritize multiple tasks with competing deadlines.

Example answer: "In my previous job, I had to manage multiple projects with competing deadlines. To prioritize the tasks, I first assessed the urgency and importance of each task and created a timeline for each project. I then communicated the timeline and priorities to my colleagues and worked with them to ensure we had a clear plan and accountability for each project. I also managed my time effectively, using tools like to-do lists and calendars to ensure I stayed on track. By being organized and proactive, I was able to meet all the deadlines and deliver high-quality work on each project."

Can you tell me about a time when you had to lead a team or take charge of a project?

Example answer: "In my previous job, I had to take charge of a project where our team was behind schedule and struggling to meet our goals. To lead the team, I first established clear communication channels and defined each team member's roles and responsibilities. I also motivated and encouraged my team members, recognizing their contributions and providing constructive feedback. I worked with my team to identify any issues or obstacles and developed solutions to overcome them. By being proactive and communicative, I was able to lead the team to success and deliver the project on time and on budget."

Tell me about a time when you had to overcome a difficult challenge or obstacle.

Example answer: "In my previous job, we had a project where we encountered unexpected delays and challenges that threatened our ability to meet our deadlines. To overcome the challenge, I first assessed the situation and identified the root cause of the issue. I then worked with my colleagues to develop a plan to mitigate the issue and minimize any further delays. I also communicated regularly with our clients to keep them informed and manage their expectations. By being proactive and resilient, we were able to overcome the challenge and deliver the project successfully."

Can you tell me about a time when you had to deal with a stressful situation at work?

Example answer: "In my previous job, we had a project where we encountered unexpected setbacks and delays that caused a great deal of stress for myself and my team. To manage the stress, I first acknowledged the emotions and concerns of my team members and provided emotional support and encouragement. I also broke down the project into smaller, more manageable tasks and focused on what we could control. I used techniques like deep breathing and exercise to manage my own stress and encouraged my team members to do the same. By being proactive and supportive, we were able to manage the stress and deliver the project successfully."

Tell me about a time when you had to handle a difficult customer or client.

Example answer: "In my previous job, I had a customer who was very unhappy with our product and service. To handle the situation, I first listened to the customer's concerns and empathized with their frustration.

I then worked to understand the root cause of the issue and identified a solution that met the customer's needs. I communicated the solution clearly and regularly with the customer, keeping them informed and managing their expectations. By being proactive and customer-focused, I was able to resolve the issue and maintain a positive relationship with the customer."

Can you tell me about a time when you had to think creatively to solve a problem?

Example answer: "In my previous job, we had a project where we encountered a technical problem that we couldn't solve using conventional methods. To think creatively, I first researched alternative approaches and technologies that could potentially solve the problem. I then brainstormed with my colleagues to develop a unique solution that combined multiple technologies and approaches. We tested and refined the solution until we found a successful one. By being innovative and collaborative, we were able to solve the problem and deliver a successful project."

Tell me about a time when you had to learn a new skill or technology quickly.

Example answer: "In my previous job, we had a project where we had to use a new software program that I wasn't familiar with. To learn the software quickly, I first researched online tutorials and training resources to gain a basic understanding of the software. I then practiced using the software on sample projects and asked for feedback from my colleagues. I also reached out to the software's support team for guidance and support. By being proactive and dedicated, I was able to quickly learn the software and use it effectively in the project."

Can you tell me about a time when you had to provide constructive feedback to a colleague or team member?

Example answer: "In my previous job, I had a colleague who was struggling with a particular task that was impacting the overall success of the project. To provide constructive feedback, I first approached the situation with empathy and understanding. I then provided specific examples of the issue and offered suggestions and guidance for improvement. I also asked for the colleague's perspectives and collaborated with them to develop a plan for improvement. By being supportive and constructive, I was able to help the colleague improve and achieve success in the project."

Tell me about a time when you had to adapt to a new work environment or culture.

Example answer: "In my previous job, I was relocated to a new office in a different country with a different work culture. To adapt to the new environment, I first researched the local work culture and etiquette to understand the norms and expectations. I also reached out to my colleagues for guidance and support and actively sought out opportunities to participate in cultural events and activities. By being open-minded and proactive, I was able to adapt quickly to the new work environment and culture."

CHAPTER SEVEN

VII. Conclusion

In conclusion, Behavioral Interview Questions are an essential part of the job interview process. They help employers understand how a candidate has handled specific situations in the past and predict how they might behave in similar situations in the future. This book has provided an in-depth overview of Behavioral Interview Questions and their importance, types, and key examples. It has also provided tips and techniques to help you prepare and answer these questions effectively.

Remember that the key to answering Behavioral Interview Questions is to be specific, detailed, and positive. Use the STAR method to structure your answers and focus on the outcome of the situation. By doing so, you can demonstrate your skills and experience in the best possible light and increase your chances of landing the job.

CHAPTER EIGHT

Final advice for preparing for Behavioral Interview Questions

As a final piece of advice for preparing for Behavioral Interview Questions, I would recommend the following:

Research the company and industry: Get to know the company's mission, values, and culture, as well as the industry trends and challenges. This will help you tailor your answers to the specific needs and expectations of the organization.

Review the job description: Pay close attention to the required skills and qualifications, as well as the duties and responsibilities of the role. This will help you identify which Behavioral Interview Questions are most likely to be asked and prepare your answers accordingly.

Practice with a friend or mentor: Ask someone you trust to simulate a job interview and ask you Behavioral Interview Questions. This will help you practice your responses, receive feedback, and identify areas for improvement.

Reflect on your past experiences: Think back to your past work, volunteer, or personal experiences and identify situations where you demonstrated the required skills and qualities. Use these examples to answer Behavioral Interview Questions and provide evidence of your abilities.

By following these steps and preparing thoroughly, you can approach Behavioral Interview Questions with confidence and demonstrate your skills and experience to potential employers.

CHAPTER NINE

Additional resources for job seekers

There are many resources available for job seekers who want to prepare for Behavioral Interview Questions and improve their job search skills. Here are some additional resources you may find helpful:

- Online courses: Websites like Coursera, Udemy, and LinkedIn Learning offer a variety of courses and tutorials on job search skills, including interviewing and communication.
- Job search books: There are many books available on job searching and interviewing, such as "What Color Is Your Parachute?" by Richard N. Bolles and "The Ultimate Job Hunter's Guidebook" by Susan Greene.
- Career counseling services: Many universities and community organizations offer free or low-cost career counseling services, which can provide one-on-one support and guidance on job searching and interviewing.
- Online forums and groups: Joining online forums or social media groups related to your industry or job search can provide a wealth of information and support from other job seekers and industry professionals.
- Professional associations: Joining a professional association related to your field can provide networking opportunities, job listings, and professional development resources.
- Remember, job searching can be a challenging process, but with the right resources and support, you can increase your chances of success and find a job that fits your skills and interests.

We hope that this book has provided you with the knowledge and confidence to excel in your next job interview. Good luck!

Note: All our books will be found by entering the name of the author Chetan Singh in the online store available in your country.

Our books are available in e-book, print paperback and handbook formats on all platforms such as Amazon, Barnes & Noble, Google Play Books Store, Apple Books Store, Kindle, Kobo, Scribd, Smashwords, Overdrive, Tolino, Vivilio and online libraries, etc.

Thank you

9 798890 024671

Printed by Libri Plureos GmbH in Hamburg,
Germany